I0019397

Alex vijay raj Amalaraj
Xiaorong Zhang

Real-time hand gesture recognition - sign language to voice conversion

Alex vijay raj Amalaraj
Xiaorong Zhang

Real-time hand gesture recognition - sign language to voice conversion

LAP LAMBERT Academic Publishing

Imprint

Any brand names and product names mentioned in this book are subject to trademark, brand or patent protection and are trademarks or registered trademarks of their respective holders. The use of brand names, product names, common names, trade names, product descriptions etc. even without a particular marking in this work is in no way to be construed to mean that such names may be regarded as unrestricted in respect of trademark and brand protection legislation and could thus be used by anyone.

Cover image: www.ingimage.com

Publisher:
LAP LAMBERT Academic Publishing
is a trademark of
International Book Market Service Ltd., member of OmniScriptum Publishing Group
17 Meldrum Street, Beau Bassin 71504, Mauritius

ISBN: 978-3-659-75671-9

Copyright © Alex vijay raj Amalaraj, Xiaorong Zhang
Copyright © 2015 International Book Market Service Ltd., member of OmniScriptum Publishing Group

ACKNOWLEDGEMENTS

"எல்லாப் புகழும் இறைவனுக்கே"

Which means "All Glory be to God" in Tamil. I would like to thank my parents Amalaraj and Nilani for their love and support without which I would not have reached this place where I am now. I thank my sister Sherly for her constant love and affection.

I extend my warmest thanks to my principal advisor, Dr. Xiaorong Zhang. Her patient guidance and encouragement have shaped and defined my research. I am very grateful to have had the opportunity to do my Thesis with an outstanding professor.

I thank Dr. Zhang for serving as the chairperson of my review committee. I thank Dr. Hamid Shahnasser for serving as my committee member.

I dedicate this Thesis to my Mother who has sacrificed so much to make me the strong person I am right now and for being the iron lady in my life.

i

TABLE OF CONTENTS

LIST OF TABLES

LIST OF FIGURES

1. Introduction:

According to the National Institute on Deafness and Other Communication Disorders (NIDCD) about 8 million people in the United States have some form of language impairment. A standardized sign language system American Sign Language(ASL) has been developed to enable communication for these people. The serious limitation of this language is that it could only be communicated between people who understand the ASL and could not be used to communicate with most of the normal people who do not understand the sign language. The goal of this research is to enable the communication between people with speaking disabilities and normal people by recognizing hand gestures that represent various words and sentences in the ASL and converting the identified words and sentences to voice signals using a wearable computing system.

Computer recognition of hand gestures has been used to provide a more natural human-computer interface, allowing people to point, select or drag through a virtual screen without touching it[1]. Interactive computer games would be enhanced if the computer could understand players' hand gestures. While there are many different types of gestures, the most structured sets belong to the sign languages. In sign languages, each gesture already has an assigned meaning, and strong rules of context and grammar may be applied to make recognition tractable.

The ASL is the language of choice for most people with hearing and speaking disabilities in the United States. The ASL uses approximately 6,000 gestures[2] for common words and finger spelling for communicating obscure words or proper nouns. However, the majority of signing is with full words, allowing signed conversations to proceed at about the pace of spoken conversation. ASL's grammar allows more flexibility in word order than English and sometimes uses redundancy for emphasis.

Different techniques have been developed to perform hand gesture recognition including leap motion sensing[3], image / video processing technique[2], recognition based on bioelectric signals such as Electromyogram(EMG)[4] and electromechanical signals such as data collected from accelerometer[5] and gyroscopes[6]. In this work, a real-time hand gesture recognition system using EMG and accelerometer is proposed and the major application is to improve the quality of life of the people with hearing and speaking disabilities.

1.1 Electromyogram(EMG):

EMG records the electrical activity of the muscle. When a muscle contracts or relaxes, there is a change in the electrical activity across the muscle. With the help of electrodes attached to the muscle, this activity can be measured and is referred as EMG. A few applications of EMG in the field of medicine includes detection of diseases that damages   muscle tissues, nerves or the junction between nerve and muscle[7]. It is also used to find the cause of weakness, paralysis or muscle twitching and for nerve conduction studies[7]. EMG is also widely used in myoelectric controlled prostheses[8] in which the EMG signals from the muscles are used to control a prosthetic device (prosthetic hand or leg).

1.2 Accelerometer:

An accelerometer is an electromechanical device that measures acceleration forces (g - forces). These g - forces may be static for example the $1g(9.8$ m/s^2) acceleration of the earth or dynamic which are caused by vibrating or moving the accelerometer. The two major applications of an accelerometer includes the detection of the orientation of the device[9] from static g - forces and the detection of the direction of the motion of the device[10] using dynamic g - forces.

1.3 Pattern recognition algorithm:

Pattern recognition(PR) is a branch of machine learning that focuses on the recognition of patterns and regularities in data. In hand gesture recognition[1], the data obtained from the gesture is processed using this algorithm to obtain the output. There are two important phases in the pattern recognition algorithm which are training and testing. Training is the initial process by which the algorithm receives a set of training examples. Each training example include an input object(data) and a desired output(hand gesture). Now the classifier which was formed from training will be able to detect what type of hand gesture any input data corresponds to, based on the training it went through. Testing refers to the process of detecting the type of hand gesture by the classifier by giving different sets of test data as input. In this particular design such a similar algorithm is implemented as it requires gestures to be detected.

1.4 Current trends and technology:

There have been different techniques for hand gesture recognition. The common feature in all the techniques is that there is an input method through which the hand gesture is captured as different forms of data and a pattern recognition algorithm that processes the data to give a recognized gesture as output. Existing data recording methods include leap motion sensing[3], image/video processing[2], accelerometer[5], gyroscope[6], data gloves[1] and EMG[4]. Existing classification algorithms used for hand gesture recognition include linear discriminant analysis[11], quadratic discriminant analysis[12], maximum entropy classifier[13], decision tree[14], kernel estimation[15], naive Bayes classifier[16], neural networks[17], support vector machines[13] and gene expression programming[18]. Similarly, the common output of all the hand gesture recognition systems is usually used to control a mechanical device or a computer application such as a GUI or a computer game. For example, EMG pattern recognition has been widely studied for neural-control of prostheses[8]. In this technique a mechanical device (a prosthetic arm or leg) is controlled by the EMG signals recorded from the user's residual muscles.

Hand gesture recognition has also been studied by several research groups for sign language recognition. A research[3] focuses mainly on leap motion sensing and compares the data collected using that particular technique by processing with two different types of classifiers. Leap motion sensor is a compact and affordable sensor for hand and finger movements in 3D space. The sensor reports data such as position and speed of the palm and fingers based on the sensor's coordinate system. The classification algorithms compared are neural networks and state vector machines. There are several inaccuracies because of the input data from the leap motion sensor being inadequate to different hand gestures.

Image/video processing[2] is a widely researched topic for sign language recognition. The classification algorithms commonly used are artificial neural networks and LBG vector quantization. These techniques for sign language detection using image processing are highly accurate but requires a camera in front of the user. This makes this technique less usable for practical purposes.

The next technique uses EMG signals from the hand muscles and accelerometer data from a device connected to the forearm for sign language recognition. One study[5] compared between wrist actions, individual finger actions and multi finger actions within sign language. The classification algorithm used was the Linear Bayesian classifier. The results compared the accuracies obtained for same gestures with conditions like EMG alone, accelerometer alone and the combination of EMG and accelerometer. It was concluded that the combination of EMG and accelerometer for hand gesture recognition was more accurate.

Another research[19] tailored to the Chinese sign language was conducted to recognize basic words, based on one-handed motions was performed. The classification algorithm used was the hierarchical decision tree. The study compared the use of EMG alone, accelerometer alone and the combination of the two for the chosen gestures. It was concluded that the combination of EMG and accelerometer for sign language recognition was more accurate.

One of the limitations of current studies[3,4,5,8,19] is that the number of investigated hand gestures are still limited. In addition, the ASL requires both hands to perform most of the gestures and the current studies have not considered two-hand gestures. Furthermore, a practical application should be able to perform real-time. None of the current techniques has investigated the real-time processing capability of the developed systems. To address these limitations, a real-time system capable of handling both one-handed and two-handed gestures is proposed in this study.

2. Methodology and Approach:

In hand gesture recognition systems, hand gestures first need to be recorded by a data collection system and then processed by a pattern recognition algorithm to generate an output decision i.e. the recognized gesture.

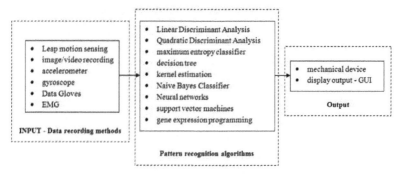

Fig. 1 Methodology - hand recognition algorithms

As shown in Fig.1 hand gesture recognition consists of three important stages namely an input stage for data collection, a processing stage which executes a pattern recognition algorithm and an output stage which displays the result. The commonly used input data collection techniques include leap motion sensing[3], image/video recording[2], accelerometer[5], gyroscope[6], data gloves[1] and EMG[8]. The pattern recognition algorithm is implemented in a processor which differs by application and the processing power required. The commonly used pattern recognition techniques are shown in the Fig.1. Based on the type of application the output of the system might be used to control a mechanical device[8] or a GUI that displays the output.

The method employed in this work to achieve hand gesture recognition is the combination of surface electromyography (sEMG) and 3-axis accelerometer. These data are collected from a device called Shimmer. The type of pattern recognition technique employed is the Linear discriminant analysis[11] and the output is displayed in a GUI.

Data is transmitted from the Shimmer device using Bluetooth to a laptop which has Matlab installed on it. The LDA algorithm is implemented in Matlab which processes the data, classifies the result and displays the output on the screen.

2.1 Shimmer:

Shimmer is a device used to collect raw EMG data and accelerometer data from the hand from which gestures are to be measured. Shimmer is a self contained device that has an inbuilt accelerometer, gyroscope, EMG sensors and much more which are controlled by a microcontroller. Data sensed by these modules can be transmitted through Bluetooth to a PC running Matlab or an Android device.

Fig. 2 Shimmer unit

Each Shimmer device can support 2 channels of EMG and a 3-axis accelerometer. Electrodes are placed in the arm as shown in Fig. 2. One channel of electrodes are placed in the Extensor digitorum muscle and the other is placed over the Flexor digitorum. The Shimmer unit is placed near the wrist so that it can measure the accelerometer activity.

A laptop with Matlab installed is used to control the shimmer unit to measure data. The program executes and communicates with the shimmer device using Bluetooth. Only the two channels of EMG and the accelerometer is allowed to transmit data, while the other sensors are turned off. This enables a decent frequency of data transfer. The data received at the laptop is stored in text files as per the sample and the gesture performed.

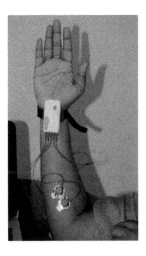

Fig. 3 placement of electrodes

2.2 Pattern recognition algorithm:

In this work Linear discriminant analysis (LDA) is adopted for classification because of its high efficiency and accuracy when compared to the other complex classifiers[11,13,16,17]. For a fixed frame size, 11 features are calculated for the EMG signal and 2 features are calculated for the accelerometer signal. These features are extracted for each window separately and are combined to form the feature matrix.

The major task of the training procedure is to calculate the mean vector for each class, the common covariance matrix and the inverse matrix. Similarly, feature matrix for the test data is also formed and both the feature matrices are loaded to the classifier. The classifier then compares the test vectors to the loaded train vector and yields a decision. The decision is one among the classes. The decision that was made is displayed in the Matlab window using an image display function.

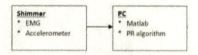

Fig. 4 Block diagram

2.3 Feature Extraction:

The Pattern recognition Algorithm uses a moving window technique. The Entire dataset is divided into different sizes depending on the Window length and the window increment size. The window increment size is chosen less than the window length such that there is a overlap in two successive windows and this is also called as overlapping window technique.

The different datasets used in this project are the two channels of EMG and the three axes accelerometer. For EMG, since it is a complex signal 11 features are extracted per channel and for accelerometer 2 features are extracted per axes. Therefore there are totally 28 features extracted per window for the two channel EMG and three axes accelerometer. The details of the different types of features used in the algorithm is explained as follows.

2.3.1 Mean Absolute Value(MAV):

MAV is the average of the absolute value of EMG signal amplitude. It is defined as

$$MAV = \frac{1}{N} \sum_{n=1}^{N} |x_n|$$

where, x_n represents EMG signal in a window and N denotes the window length.

2.3.2 Standard Deviation(SD):

SD captures the power of the EMG signal as a feature.

$$SD = \sqrt{\frac{1}{N-1} \sum_{n=1}^{N} (x_n - \bar{x})^2}$$

2.3.3 <u>Waveform Length(WL)</u>:

Waveform length is the cumulative length of the waveform over time segment. WL is similar to waveform amplitude, frequency and time. The WL can be formulated as

$$WL = \sum_{n=1}^{N-1} |x_{n+1} - x_n|$$

2.3.4 <u>Zero Crossing</u>:

ZC is the number of times the EMG signal crosses zero in x-axis.

2.3.5 <u>Turns</u>:

Turns refer to the number of changes between the positive and negative slope of an EMG signal.

2.3.6 <u>Integral Absolute Value(IAV)</u>:

This is similar to MAV but the mean is not taken.

$$IAV = \sum_{n=1}^{N} |x_n|$$

2.3.7 <u>Root Mean Square(RMS)</u>:

RMS is related to constant force and non-fatiguing contraction. RMS is defined as

$$RMS = \sqrt{\frac{1}{N}\sum_{n=1}^{N} x_n^2}$$

where, x_n represents EMG signal in a window and N denotes the window length.

2.3.8 Auto Regression(AR):

AR model describes each sample of EMG signals as a linear combination of previous EMG samples(x_{n-i}) plus a white noise error term (w_n). In addition, p is the order of the AR model. AR coefficients(α_i) are used as features in EMG hand movement recognition. The definition of AR model is given by

$$x_n = -\sum_{i=1}^{p} \alpha_i x_{n-i} + w_n$$

In this project 4th order AR is implemented.

3. Experimental Protocol:

Sensors were placed in both hands on specific muscle locations. The muscles that were chosen are the flexor digitorum and the extensor digitorum. The initial idea was to create a real-time system that is capable to train and test hand gestures in real-time. To achieve this individual blocks were created one by one in Matlab. The first block was created as the training phase. As shown in Fig. 5, training starts with the first gesture

14

being held by the hand with the shimmer device. For each training set there were totally 3 trials and data from the same gesture will be collected three times. Each trial will be for 2 seconds and each trial will be recorded in different text files. The frequency at which data is recorded is 512Hz.

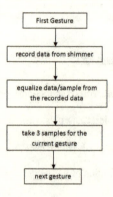

Fig.5 Training block diagram

After which, the text files are opened again to equalize the number of data lines in each text file. Then the same procedure is repeated three times for the same gesture. Once a gesture is finished, a text is displayed instructing the user to change the current gesture to the next gesture. When the user changes the gesture and inputs 'yes' to the system, the same procedure is repeated until all gestures are successfully trained.

After the collection of data for the all gestures, the training algorithm for pattern recognition is called. The collected data is given as input to the training part of the pattern recognition algorithm. The algorithm creates a feature matrix based on the data samples given as input. This is followed by the classifier training, which includes LDA training.

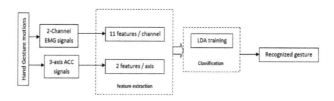

Fig. 6 PR algorithm Block diagram

LDA training includes the formation of the feature vector followed by its normalization followed by the actual training part and the calculation of accuracy. The following code snippet shows a brief outline of the training algorithm.

```
for j=1:length(file)
    TrainFeature=[TrainFeature,Feature_matrix(j).feat];
    TrainClass=[TrainClass,j*ones(1,size(Feature_matrix(j).feat,2))];
end
[TrainFeature,PS.set]=mapstd(TrainFeature); % normalize the feature vector
total_win_num = size(TrainFeature,2);   %total number of windows in the training dataset

[Wg, Cg]=LDA_train(TrainFeature,TrainClass,total_win_num,CLASS); % LDA training

train_accuracy = LDA_train_accuracy(TrainFeature,TrainClass,total_win_num,CLASS, Wg, Cg);
```

Fig. 7 LDA training - code snippet

The inputs to the LDA_Train function include the TrainFeature which is the feature matrix of the training data. The next input is the TrainClass which is the class label for the feature matrix. The other inputs include the total number of windows and the number of classes. The outputs from the LDA_Train function include Wg and Cg which are the two parameters of the LDA classifier. This is followed by the calculation of train accuracy. Train accuracy is calculated by dividing the number of correct decisions by the total number of windows.

Once the Training accuracy has been calculated, the code enters the Testing phase. In this phase the shimmer is triggered only once and the device continuously samples EMG and accelerometer data and sends it to the laptop through Bluetooth unless a hardware interrupt is triggered. The data from the shimmer device is continuously sent through the testing algorithm to form decisions. Similar to the testing phase, the Raw data is sent to the tdfeats function to form a feature matrix with the four time domain functions. Then these feature are normalized. Followed by normalization, the LDA_test function is used for classification. The classifier compares the feature matrices of both the testing and the training phases and gives out a class as a decision. The decision is one of the classes from the training.

Once the decision is obtained, the decision is displayed in the Matlab window as numbers. Also, the imshow function of Matlab which displays images is used to visually display an image based on the test decision. The procedure explained above is the same for all experiments. Each individual experiments were conducted with different gestures and the results are obtained as follows.

3.1 Experiment 1:

The American sign language has different types of gestures starting from single handed, two handed to wrist motions and so on. The main objective of this first experiment is to choose hand motions that look similar and to test the classifier's accuracy for those motions. So, the 26 alphabets in the ASL were chosen as gestures for this experiment. They are single handed motions and are mainly finger based motions i.e., they are placed in the same location but only differ by differences in the position of the fingers. The total number of classes in this experiment is 26, all the alphabets in the ASL. The gestures for this experiment are shown in the following figures.

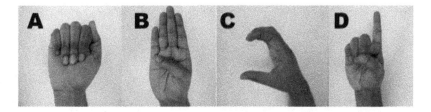

Fig. 8 Experiment 1 Gestures - A, B, C, D

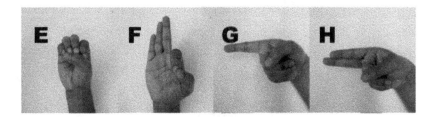

Fig. 9 Experiment 1 Gestures - E, F, G, H

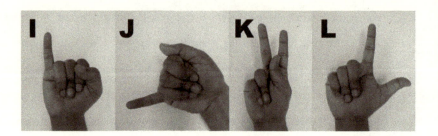

Fig. 10 Experiment 1 Gestures - I, J, K, L

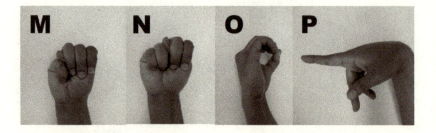

Fig.11 Experiment 1 Gestures - M, N, O, P

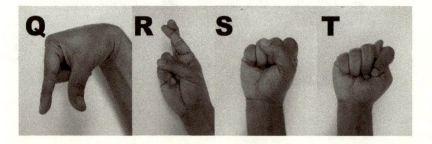

Fig.12 Experiment 1 Gestures - Q, R, S, T

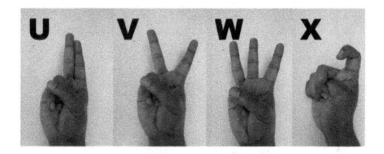

Fig.13 Experiment 1 Gestures - U, V, W, X

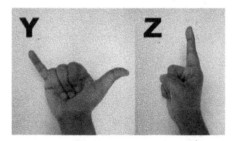

Fig.14 Experiment 1 Gestures - Y, Z

The experiment begins by collecting first set of samples for all the 26 classes. Each sample lasts for 2 seconds and is saved in a text file. Then the second set of data are collected for all the 26 classes followed by the third set. Once the third set is collected, the Pattern recognition algorithm is trained with the three samples for all the 26 classes.

The PR algorithm uses a moving window technique by which it divides the entire data into number of windows based on the window length which is 160 in this case. Then based on the window increment size (20) the window moves by 20 values and the next set of 160 values are used. Features are extracted for each window, feature matrix is formed and the algorithm continues the training procedure. As soon as the training is over, three more samples per class are collected in the same way and this corresponds to the test data. This test data is fed into the PR algorithm to check for accuracy. Accuracy is calculated by dividing the total number of windows by the number of correct windows and the test accuracy is displayed. With this accuracy the performance of the Classifier for this particular experiment can be evaluated.

As the experiment was performed, it was noted that the accuracy improved with increase in the window length and the window increment. So the experiment for different window lengths and different window increment sizes was also performed.

3.2 Experiment 2:

The next experiment included common words from the ASL which require only one hand to perform. Instead of choosing a lot of words, only four words were chosen. During the selection of these words it was made sure that they were commonly used and they look very similar and there was a possibility for the PR algorithm to confuse with these words. This represented a worst case scenario of the project. The gestures that represented the words are boy, girl, dad and mom as shown in the following figures. The same testing and training procedure used in experiment 1 was repeated but only with a difference of 5 classes. The classes include boy, girl, dad, mom and no move. The no move gesture corresponds to no movement of the hand and is considered as a rest position. This is added to the training set for the classifier to understand the rest position before and after each gesture is performed. And hence, the training and testing accuracy for this experiment was found.

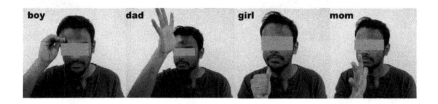

Fig.15 Experiment 2 Gestures - boy, dad, girl, mom

3.3 Experiment 3:

This experiment was performed to accommodate two hand motions in to the system. Three two hand motions along with two one hand motions were used in this experiment. The one hand motions in this experiment were performed with the other hand at rest. The two hand motions represent Marriage, Husband and Wife in ASL and the one hand motions represent boy and girl in ASL. As shown in the figures below all these hand gestures are similar to one another and this constitutes as a worst case scenario. Both the training and testing procedure were performed similar to experiment 1 with 6 classes including one class for no motion in which both the hands are placed in a rest position. When the testing process is over the accuracy for this experiment was found.

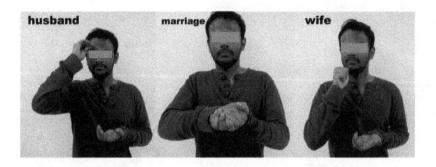

Fig.16 Experiment 3 Gestures - husband, marriage, wife

3.4 <u>Experiment 4</u>:

The next step in the project is to add some basic sentences that could be formed with the words chosen. As a first step 7 classes were chosen to form a basic sentence 'My name is ALEX'. The 7 classes are A, E, L, my, name, X and no move. These classes are formed with one hand motions. The training procedure was done similar to the first experiment and the words were not trained in the order of the sentence. The accuracy obtained was recorded.

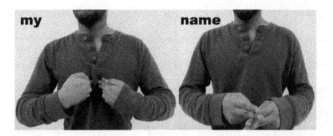

Fig.17 Experiment 4 Gestures - my, name

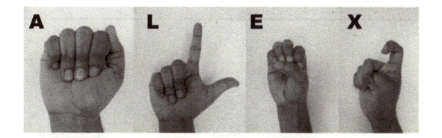

Fig.18 Experiment 4 Gestures - A, L, E, X

3.5 <u>Experiment 5</u>:

The main aim of this experiment is to choose words that could form a few basic sentences. For this purpose 11 words were chosen which could be used to form a series of different basic sentences. Some of the words required two hand motions and hence this experiment was based on two hand motions. The 12 classes in this experiment are What, you, How, dad, mom, my, name, A, L, E, X and no move. These words can form up to 9 basic sentences including,

1. My name is Alex

2. What is your name?

3. What is your Dad's name?

4. What is your Mom's name?

5. How are you?

6. How is your Dad?

7. How is your Mom?

8. How is Alex?

9. What are you?

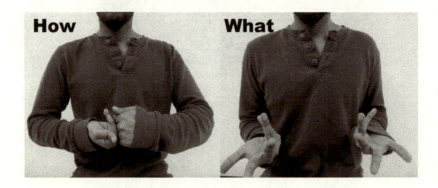

Fig.19 Experiment 5 Gestures - how, what

Fig.20 Experiment 5 Gestures - dad, mom, you

Fig.21 Experiment 5 Gestures - my, name

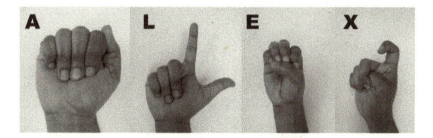

Fig.22 Experiment 5 Gestures - A, L, E, X

The sentences mentioned are just examples of what could be formed from the words used in this experiment. The training and the testing procedure was similar to that of the first experiment and the accuracy obtained was recorded.

3.6 Experiment 6:

This experiment was similar to the previous experiment but the aim was to add more classes and thereby forming more basic sentences. Since some of the classes required two hand motions this experiment also used data from both the hands for processing. The number of classes in this experiment was 21. The words represented by the classes are What, you, How, dad, mom, my, name, A, L, E, X, husband, wife, like, feel, hot, cold, happy, angry, cry and no move. There are more than 54 basic sentences that could be formed by these 21 classes and they are listed below.

1. My name is Alex

2. Are you Alex?

3. How is Alex?

4. My Dad's name is Alex

5. My Mom's name is Alex

6. My Husband's name is Alex

7. My Wife's name is Alex

8. Alex is hot

9. Alex is cold

10. Alex is happy

11. Alex is angry

12. Alex is crying

13. What is your name?

14. What is your Dad's name?

15. What is your Mom's name?

16. What is your Wife's name?

17. What is your Husband's name?

18. How are you?

19. How is your Dad?

20. How is your Mom?

21. How is your Husband?

22. How is your wife?

23. How is Alex?

24. What are you?

25. How do you feel?

26. How does your Dad feel?

27. How does your Mom feel?

28. How does your Husband feel?

29. How does your Wife feel?

30. I feel hot

31. I feel Cold

32. I am Happy

33. I am angry

34. My dad feels hot

35. My dad feels cold

36. My dad is happy

37. My dad is angry

38. My mom feels hot

39. My mom feels cold

40. My mom is happy

41. My mom is angry

42. My husband feels hot

43. My husband feels cold

44. My husband is happy

45. My husband is angry

46. My wife feels hot

47. My wife feels cold

48. My wife is happy

49. My wife is angry

50. I am crying

51. My dad is crying

52. My mom is crying

53. My husband is crying

54. My wife is crying

Fig.23 Experiment 6 Gesture - no_move

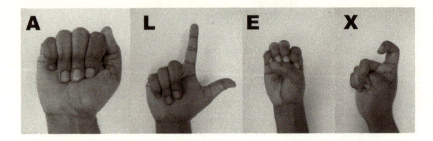

Fig.24 Experiment 6 Gesture - A, L, E, X

Fig.25 Experiment 6 Gesture - angry, cold, cry

Fig.26 Experiment 6 Gesture - dad, mom, you

Fig.27 Experiment 6 Gesture - Feel, hot, like

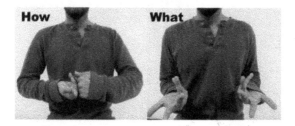

Fig.28 Experiment 6 Gesture - how, what

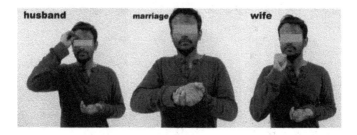

Fig.29 Experiment 6 Gesture - husband, marriage, wife

Fig.30 Experiment 6 Gesture - my, name

The sentences mentioned are just examples of what could be formed from the words used in this experiment. The training and the testing procedures were performed similar to the first experiment and the results obtained were recorded.

4. Results:

The main objective of this work is to form the skeleton of a Real-time Hand gesture recognition system that can be used for sign language to voice conversion. The skeleton consists of an EMG and Accelerometer collection system and a Pattern recognition algorithm which classifies the data received and gives decisions as output.

The existing time domain features that are used in the pattern recognition algorithm[20] are mean absolute value, waveform length, zero count and number of slope sign changes. After careful analysis of the data, time-frequency domain features were added to the algorithm. The features include Root mean square, Integral absolute value, Autoregressive feature and Cepstral coefficients. This complex algorithm is required only for EMG signal processing and the accelerometer signal requires only 2 features extracted from it including the Mean absolute value and the standard deviation.

With this algorithm, there were 6 experiments conducted as shown in the working section. The results from these experiments were recorded and are shown below.

4.1 Experiment 1:

This experiment was performed with 26 alphabets at the same time. It was noted that the accuracies varied with the change in window length and window size. So these changes were recorded in the table shown below.

Table. 1 Experiment 1 - Result

	$W_L = 160; W_{Inc} = 20$	$W_L = 320; W_{Inc} = 40$	$W_L = 500; W_{Inc} = 50$	$W_L = 800; W_{Inc} = 80$
Test accuracy	78.52 %	85.95 %	87.69 %	88.46 %
Train accuracy	87.93 %	96.15 %	98.63 %	100 %

Table.2 Confusion matrix for Classes A to I

	A	B	C	D	E	F	G	H	I
A	96.23	0.00	0.00	0.00	0.00	0.00	0.00	0.00	0.00
B	0.00	83.65	1.26	0.00	0.00	0.00	0.00	0.00	6.92
C	0.00	7.55	59.75	12.58	0.00	0.63	0.00	1.26	1.26
D	0.00	0.00	18.87	64.78	0.00	0.00	0.00	0.00	4.40
E	0.00	0.00	0.00	0.00	97.48	0.00	0.00	0.00	0.00
F	0.00	1.89	0.00	0.00	0.00	89.94	0.00	0.00	4.40
G	0.00	0.00	1.89	5.66	0.00	0.00	58.49	29.56	0.63
H	0.00	0.63	0.63	0.00	0.00	0.00	6.29	42.77	0.00
I	0.00	1.89	10.69	15.72	0.00	0.00	0.00	0.00	76.73
J	0.00	0.00	0.00	0.00	2.52	0.00	0.63	8.18	0.00

	A	B	C	D	E	F	G	H	I
K	3.14	0.00	1.26	0.00	0.00	0.00	23.90	0.00	1.26
L	0.00	0.00	0.00	0.00	0.00	0.00	0.00	0.00	0.00
M	0.00	0.00	0.00	0.00	0.00	0.00	0.00	0.00	0.00
N	0.00	0.00	1.89	0.00	0.00	0.00	0.00	0.00	0.00
O	0.00	0.00	0.00	0.00	0.00	0.00	0.00	0.00	0.00
P	0.00	0.00	0.00	0.00	0.00	0.00	0.00	0.00	0.00
Q	0.00	4.40	3.77	1.26	0.00	4.40	0.63	2.52	4.40
R	0.00	0.00	0.00	0.00	0.00	0.00	0.00	0.00	0.00
S	0.00	0.00	0.00	0.00	0.00	0.00	0.00	0.00	0.00
T	0.00	0.00	0.00	0.00	0.00	0.00	3.77	6.29	0.00
U	0.00	0.00	0.00	0.00	0.00	0.00	5.03	9.43	0.00
V	0.00	0.00	0.00	0.00	0.00	3.14	0.00	0.00	0.00
W	0.00	0.00	0.00	0.00	0.00	0.00	1.26	0.00	0.00
X	0.63	0.00	0.00	0.00	0.00	0.00	0.00	0.00	0.00
Y	0.00	0.00	0.00	0.00	0.00	0.00	0.00	0.00	0.00

[ ] ⟶ Accuracy of the same class in %

[ ] ⟶ Accuracy of the other class that it got confused with the most in %

Table.3 Confusion matrix for Classes J to R

	J	K	L	M	N	O	P	Q	R
A	0.00	0.00	0.00	0.00	0.00	0.00	0.00	0.00	0.00
B	0.00	0.00	0.00	0.00	0.00	0.00	0.00	0.63	0.00
C	0.00	0.00	0.00	0.00	1.26	0.00	0.00	7.55	0.00
D	0.00	0.00	0.00	0.00	0.00	0.00	0.00	0.63	0.00
E	0.00	0.00	0.00	0.00	0.00	0.00	0.00	0.00	0.00
F	0.00	0.00	0.00	0.00	0.63	0.00	0.00	0.63	0.00
G	0.00	14.47	0.00	0.00	0.00	0.00	0.00	0.00	0.00
H	0.00	0.00	0.00	0.00	0.00	0.00	0.00	10.06	0.00
I	0.00	0.00	0.00	0.00	0.00	0.00	0.00	1.26	0.00
J	94.34	0.00	0.00	0.00	0.00	15.09	0.00	0.00	0.00
K	0.00	84.28	0.00	0.00	0.00	0.00	0.00	0.00	0.00
L	0.00	0.00	92.45	3.77	0.00	0.00	0.00	0.00	0.00
M	0.00	0.00	7.55	96.23	0.00	0.00	0.00	0.00	0.00
N	0.00	0.00	0.00	0.00	86.79	0.00	0.00	15.72	0.00
O	2.52	0.00	0.00	0.00	0.00	83.02	2.52	0.00	0.63
P	0.00	0.00	0.00	0.00	0.00	0.63	89.31	0.00	15.72
Q	0.00	0.00	0.00	0.00	6.29	0.00	0.00	55.35	0.00
R	0.00	0.00	0.00	0.00	0.00	1.26	5.03	0.00	72.96
S	0.00	0.00	0.00	0.00	0.00	0.00	3.14	0.00	5.03
T	3.14	0.00	0.00	0.00	0.00	0.00	0.00	0.00	0.00
U	0.00	0.00	0.00	0.00	0.00	0.00	0.00	0.00	0.00
V	0.00	0.00	0.00	0.00	5.03	0.00	0.00	8.18	0.00

	J	K	L	M	N	O	P	Q	R
W	0.00	1.26	0.00	0.00	0.00	0.00	0.00	0.00	5.66
X	0.00	0.00	0.00	0.00	0.00	0.00	0.00	0.00	0.00
Y	0.00	0.00	0.00	0.00	0.00	0.00	0.00	0.00	0.00

⟶ Accuracy of the same class in %

⟶ Accuracy of the other class that it got confused with the most in %

Table.4 Confusion matrix for Classes S to Z

	S	T	U	V	W	X	Y	Z
A	0.00	0.00	0.00	0.00	8.81	9.43	0.00	0.00
B	0.00	0.00	0.00	0.00	0.00	0.00	0.00	0.00
C	0.00	0.63	3.14	0.00	0.00	0.00	0.00	0.00
D	0.00	0.00	2.52	0.00	0.00	0.00	0.00	0.00
E	0.00	0.00	0.00	0.00	0.00	0.00	0.00	0.00
F	0.00	0.00	3.77	0.63	0.00	0.00	0.00	3.77
G	0.00	15.09	6.92	0.00	0.00	0.00	0.00	0.00
H	0.00	20.13	11.32	0.00	0.00	0.00	0.00	0.00
I	0.00	0.00	0.00	0.00	0.00	0.63	0.00	0.00
J	0.00	5.03	11.32	0.00	0.00	0.00	0.00	0.00
K	0.00	1.89	1.26	0.00	2.52	0.00	0.00	0.00
L	0.63	0.00	0.00	0.00	0.00	0.00	0.00	0.00
M	0.63	0.00	0.00	0.00	0.00	0.00	0.00	0.00

	S	T	U	V	W	X	Y	Z
N	0.00	0.00	0.00	7.55	0.00	0.00	0.00	0.00
O	0.63	0.00	0.00	0.00	0.00	0.00	0.00	0.00
P	20.13	0.00	0.00	0.00	0.00	0.00	0.00	0.00
Q	0.00	2.52	7.55	1.26	0.00	0.00	0.00	0.00
R	5.66	0.00	0.00	0.00	7.55	0.00	0.00	0.00
S	72.33	0.00	0.00	0.00	0.00	0.00	0.00	0.00
T	0.00	53.46	16.35	0.00	0.00	0.00	0.00	0.00
U	0.00	0.63	35.85	1.89	0.00	0.00	0.00	0.00
V	0.00	0.00	0.00	88.68	0.00	0.00	0.00	0.63
W	0.00	0.63	0.00	0.00	81.13	0.00	0.00	0.00
X	0.00	0.00	0.00	0.00	0.00	89.94	0.00	0.00
Y	0.00	0.00	0.00	0.00	0.00	0.00	100.00	0.00

[ ] ⟶ Accuracy of the same class in %

[ ] ⟶ Accuracy of the other class that it got confused with the most in %

4.2 Experiment 2:

This experiment used simple words like boy, girl, dad, mom and no move. Both the test and the train accuracy obtained was 100%.

Table.5 Experiment 2 - Result

Parameter	Value
Channels	5
Class	5
Window Increment size	20
Window length	160
Test accuracy	100%
Total window number	795
Test number correct	795
Train accuracy	100%

4.3 Experiment 3:

A set of 5 signs which utilizes both the hands to perform the gesture was chosen for this experiment. The signs represents Marriage, Husband, wife, boy, girl and no move. The test accuracy was 99.9 % and the train accuracy was 100 % for this experiment.

Table.6 Experiment 3 - Result

Parameter	Value
Channels	10
Class	6
Window Increment size	20
Window length	160
Test accuracy	99.9%
Total window number	954
Test number correct	953
Train accuracy	100%

4.4 Experiment 4:

Signs that represent words that can form basic sentences were considered for this experiment. The words that were chosen are A, E, L, my, name, X and no move. The sentence that could be formed from these words is My name is ALEX. The test accuracy was 96.59 % and the train accuracy was 98.2 % for this experiment.

Table.7 Experiment 4 - Result

Parameter	Value
Channels	5
Class	7
Window Increment size	20
Window length	160
Test accuracy	96.59%
Total window number	1113
Test number correct	1075
Train accuracy	98.20%

4.5 Experiment 5:

For this experiment, signs that requires both the hands were chosen. The words include What, you, How, dad, mom, my, name, A, L, E, X and no move. These words can form up to 9 basic sentences. The test accuracy was 98.95 % and the train accuracy was 100 %.

Table.8 Experiment 5 - Result

Parameter	Value
Channels	10
Class	12
Window Increment size	20
Window length	160
Test accuracy	98.95%
Total window number	1908
Test number correct	1888
Train accuracy	100%

4.6 Experiment 6:

This is similar to the previous experiment but more classes are added to form more than 50 basic sentences. The signs that represent words include What, you, How, dad, mom, my, name, A, L, E, X, husband, wife, like, feel, hot, cold, happy, angry and cry. The test accuracy was 97.6 % and train accuracy was 98.95 %.

Table.9 Experiment 6 - Result

Parameter	Value
Channels	10
Class	21
Window Increment size	20
Window length	160
Test accuracy	97.6%
Total window number	3339
Test number correct	3259
Train accuracy	98.95%

5. Future Work:

There is a huge scope for future work from this study. A major disadvantage of using the Linear discriminant analysis classifier is that it requires a lot of training time. Each and every class has to be trained for a definite period of time for it to be accurate. Work on reducing this training time could solve a lot practical problems this system has. The accuracy for the experiment which involves all the 26 alphabets in ASL was 79%. This accuracy could be improved if these 26 classes were mixed with common words.

All the experiments in this research are performed on a single participant. Different participants with different level of expertise in ASL could be included in the research and the accuracies for that could be performed. There was only one type of classification algorithm that was implemented which was the LDA. Other classification algorithms could be implemented and compared for the one with the best accuracy for this type of application.

The PR algorithm was implemented on a Laptop which makes it hard to use for practical purposes. Experiments for implementing in standalone processors or an Android device could be performed which makes the application more practical.

6. Conclusion:

This study was new in its context because it came up with a practical application that could improve the quality of life of people with speaking disabilities. If implemented as a consumer product it could be beneficial to about 8 million people in the United

States alone. A real-time system capable of converting hand gestures in the American sign language to voice signals was implemented. The EMG and accelerometer data from the hand were measured by a device called Shimmer and these were the only input data. The recorded data was transmitted through Bluetooth to a PC running Matlab in it. A Pattern recognition algorithm was implemented in Matlab which is used for processing the data. The LDA classifier is first trained with three sets of training data and then it is tested with three samples of test data from which the accuracy of the system is calculated. For a real-time performance, the decision is displayed on the screen in real-time.

The major aim of this study is to address a few issues in the current studies. One of them was to include two hand gestures since most words from ASL used two hand gestures to perform a particular sign. This study achieved an accuracy of 97.6% which had 21 two-hand gesture(words) from the ASL which can form over 54 basic sentences. Then an experiment for including all the 26 alphabets was performed. An accuracy of 78.52% was obtained and the problems with certain alphabets whose accuracies are very low are noted. Further research could be done to figure out the reason for those alphabets to have low accuracies and the techniques that could be implemented to improve them.

7. References:

[1] M. Ishikawa and H. Matsumura, Recognition of a Hand-gesture based on self organization using a Data Glove, Neural Information Processing, proceedings, International Conference on Neural Networks Information Processing(ICONIP) '99. pp 739-745, 1999.

[2] T. Starner and A. Pentland, "Real-time American sign language recognition from video using hidden Markov models", page 5B Systems and Applications, 1995.

[3] C. Chuan and E. Regina "American Sign Language recognition using leap motion sensor, Machine learning and Applications(ICMLA), 2014.

[4] X. Chen , X. Zhang , Z.-Y. Zhao , J.-H. Yang , V. Lantz and K.-Q. Wang "Multiple hand gesture recognition based on surface EMG signal", Proc. 1st Int. Conf. Bioinformatics and Biomedical Engineering, no. 6, pp.506 -509 2007

[5] X. Chen , X. Zhang , Z. Y. Zhao , J. H. Yang , V. Lantz and K. Q. Wang "Hand gesture recognition research based on surface EMG sensors and 2D-accelerometers", Proc. 11th IEEE International Symposium on wearable computers, pp.11 -14 2007

[6] A. Boschmann, B. Nofen and M. Platzner "Improving Transient state myoelectric signal recognition in hand movement classification using gyroscopes" Engineering in medicine and biology society, 2013

[7] M.J. Zwarts and D.F. Stageman "Surface EMG applications in Neurology", IEEE 2004, pp 323-342.

[8] D. Nishikawa , W. Yu , H. Yokoi and Y. Kakazu "EMG prosthetic hand controller using real-time learning method", Proc. IEEE Int. Conf. Syst., Man, Cybern., pp.I-153 -I-158 1999

[9] A. Friedman, N. Hajj Chehade, C. Chien, and G. Pottie, "Estimation of accelerometer orientation for activity recognition," in Engineering in Medicine and Biology Society (EMBC), 2012 Annual International Conference of the IEEE, pp. 2076-2079, IEEE, 2012.

[10] H. Kimura and M. Makamura "Identification method of sensor directions and sensitivities in multi- axis accelerometer", IEEE Industrial Electronics society, pg 2595 - 2600, 2012.

[11] J.A. Spanias and E.J. Perreault "Detection of and Compensation for EMG disturbances for powered lower limb prosthesis control", IEEE Transactions on Neural Systems and Rehabilitation Engineering, pp 99, 2015.

[12] Y. Kocigit and I. Kilic "Using LBG algorithm for extracting the features of EMG signals" Signal Processing, Communications and Applications Conference, 2008.

[13] J. Du and S. Wang "A systematic comparison of SVM and Maximum Entropy classifiers for translation Error detection" pg 125 - 128, International Association of Logopedics and Phoniatrics, 2012.

[14] A. Abdelhalim, I. Traore. A New Method for Learning Decision Trees from Rules. International   Conference on Machine Learning and Applications, 2009, pp.693-698.

[15] X. Yin and Z. Hao "Adaptive Kernel Density Estimation using Beta Kernel", pg 3293 - 3297, Machine learning and Cybernetics, 2007.

[16] Y. Tang, W. Pan and H. Li Fuzzy Naive Bayes classifier based on fuzzy clustering. Proceedings of 2002 IEEE International Conference on System, Man and Cybernetics (2002).

[17] H. Qiao , J. Peng , Z. B. Xu and B. Zhang "A reference model approach to stability analysis of neural networks", IEEE Trans. Syst., Man, Cybern., Prat B: Cybern., vol. 33, no. 6, pp.925 -936 2003.

[18] J. Zhang and Z. Wu "Unconstrained gene expression programming" IEEE Congress on Evolutionary Computation, 2009.

[19] X. Zhang , X. Chen , Y. Li , V. Lantz , K. Wang and J. Yang "A framework for hand gesture recognition based on accelerometer and emg sensors", IEEE Trans. Syst., Man, Cybern., A, Syst., Humans, vol. 41, no. 6, pp.1064 -1076 2011.

[20] X. Zhang and H Huang "Implementing an FPGA system for real-time intent recognition for prosthetic legs", Design Automation Conference pg 169 - 175, 2012.

I want morebooks!

Buy your books fast and straightforward online - at one of world's fastest growing online book stores! Environmentally sound due to Print-on-Demand technologies.

Buy your books online at
www.morebooks.shop

Kaufen Sie Ihre Bücher schnell und unkompliziert online – auf einer der am schnellsten wachsenden Buchhandelsplattformen weltweit! Dank Print-On-Demand umwelt- und ressourcenschonend produziert.

Bücher schneller online kaufen
www.morebooks.shop

KS OmniScriptum Publishing
Brivibas gatve 197
LV-1039 Riga, Latvia
Telefax:+371 686 204 55

info@omniscriptum.com
www.omniscriptum.com

www.ingramcontent.com/pod-product-compliance
Lightning Source LLC
LaVergne TN
LVHW042350060326
832902LV00006B/519